LIBERTY AND JUSTICE FOR ALL

Written by Shirley Neitzel

Illustrated by Carolyn R. Stich

D1500590

 River Road Publications, Inc.

ISBN: 0-938682-70-9
Text Copyright © 2002 by Shirley Neitzel
Illustrations Copyright © 2002 by Carolyn R. Stich

About the Author

Shirley Neitzel earned her BA from Eastern Michigan University with a major in Social Studies. After receiving her MA from Western Michigan University in the

Teaching of Reading she did graduate work in the field of writing. She was an elementary teacher in the Caledonia Community Schools when she began to write for children. She is the author of a number of books including the picture book *The Jacket I Wear in the Snow* and an illustrated story book of retold Ojibwa legends, *From the Land of the White Birch*. Shirley and her husband live in Grand Rapids, Michigan.

About the Illustrator

Through her detailed illustrations, Carolyn Stich has brought to life the intentions of our Founding Fathers. Her personification of core democratic values will benefit all students. Carolyn Stich lives in Holland, Michigan, with her husband and two children. Carolyn's work can be found throughout West Michigan and in *Paul Bunyan and the Winter of the Blue Snow*.

Special Thanks

A special thank you to Amy, Bobbie, Cabrey, Elli, Emma, Jayne, Leslie K., Max, Robert, Ryan, Sydney, Tori, Leslie W., Matthew P., Matthew R., and Wendy.

Contents

Liver Tea and Just This for All

Core Democratic Values
The United States is founded on values that are important to all of us as citizens.

"Wow! Look at our classroom!" said Kevin. "It looks like a flag!"

Mrs. Jordan smiled as she pinned a nametag to his shirt. "I'm glad you like it."

Kevin and Bob chose desks. Lexie sat across from Kevin and next to Kristen. "I love all the red, white, and blue stuff, don't you?"

"Yes," Kristen answered, "and I like our desks in groups instead of rows."

When all the children were sitting, the teacher said, "Welcome to Key School's Patriots. This year we'll learn about our rights and duties as citizens. Let's begin by saluting the flag. Please stand and put your right hand over your heart." Mrs. Jordan looked around. She winked at Alex. "Your other right hand." Then she began, "I pledge allegiance. . ."

The children joined in. ". . .to the flag of the United States of America, and to the Republic for which it stands, one Nation under God, indivisible, with liberty and justice for all."

When they sat down, Mrs. Jordan said, "There are some hard words in the Pledge we just said. Here is a copy for each of you." She passed papers. "In your group, talk about the words I've underlined. Then we'll see if we can figure out what the Pledge means."

Lexie giggled. "I don't know what all these words mean, but I know something the Pledge doesn't mean." She pointed to her paper. "I used to think it said, 'with *liver tea* and *just this* for all.' I didn't know what *just this* was, but I thought it would be better than *liver tea*!"

Kristen, Bob, and Kevin laughed.

Bob tapped his paper with the eraser on his pencil. "When my brother was in kindergarten he asked me, 'Where do the four witches stand?' I didn't know what he was talking about. He said his teacher told the kids to say that. Then he told me she let him hold the flag, so I figured out he meant, *for which it stands*."

The kids laughed again.

Mrs. Jordan stopped by their desks. "Which of these words do you know?" she asked.

Kristen looked up. "Liberty means to be free."

"And," said Bob, "a pledge is a promise."

"Very good," said Mrs. Jordan. "Keep up the good work."

"May we use a dictionary?" asked Kevin.

"Yes, you may." She pointed to some books on the shelf.

After a while, Mrs. Jordan asked each group to share its ideas with the class. As they gave the meanings of the words, she wrote them on the board. Then the children made suggestions for rewriting the Pledge. Mrs. Jordan wrote the new Promise on a large paper.

I promise to show respect for the flag, because it stands for our country. The United States of America is made up of fifty states  *that all work together. Each person is free to do what they want and everyone is treated fairly.*

Mrs. Jordan put down her marker. "You've done a good job! I hope this helps you understand what you are saying when we salute the flag."

"It sure does," said Bob.

The class agreed.

Kevin poked Lexie. "Our Promise is a lot easier to understand than *liver tea* and *just this* for all!"

Holly's Club

Popular Sovereignty
***People rule through their votes and
leaders listen to ideas from the people.***

"I'm starting a club," Holly said. "Want to join?"

"Sure," said Amanda. "Who's in it?"

"So far just me and you, but I'm going to ask a couple other girls. No boys!"

"Right!" Amanda giggled. "Not in our club!"

Holly waved her arm. "Hey, Kristen! Zoe! Come here!"

The girls ran over. "What's up?" asked Kristen.

"Want to join my club?"

"What's it for?" asked Zoe.

"Just for fun. We play together every recess."

"Okay," the girls agreed.

"I'm the president." Holly brushed hair from her face. "First one outside saves swings for the others."

The girls played until the bell rang.

"I like our club," said Zoe.

"Me, too!" said Kristen.

"Me, three," said Amanda.

Holly said, "Tomorrow let's all wear yellow socks."

"Why?" asked Amanda.

"To show we're a club."

"Cool," said Zoe.

The next day they each rolled up their pants to show their yellow socks. "Having a club is fun!" said Kristen.

"Yes," said Zoe. "Let's play soccer with the other kids."

"OK," said Kristen.

"No," said Holly.

"Why not?" asked Amanda.

"Because I said so."

"Let's vote," said Zoe. "Who wants to play soccer?"

"I do," said Kristen.

"Me, too," said Amanda.

"No," said Holly.

"Three to one," said Zoe. "Let's go."

Holly stamped her foot. "I said, 'No,' and I'm the president."

"That doesn't mean we have to do everything you want," said Kristen.

"Yes, you do. It's my club!"

"I thought it was our club," said Amanda.

"I don't want to be in the club if my vote doesn't count," said Kristen.

"Me neither." Zoe walked away.

Kristen and Amanda followed her.

"Too bad for you!" Holly called after them. *I'll find someone else to be in my club,* she thought.

She sat on a swing and watched her friends play soccer.

The Election

Popular Sovereignty

People vote for those who agree with them about important ideas. A representative should think about what all the people want and decide what is best for everyone.

One morning the children read a note on the board: STUDENT COUNCIL ELECTION TODAY!

"What's student council?" asked Zoe.

"They plan neat things," said Kevin.

"Like what?"

"Fun stuff and parties."

"I'd like that," said Holly.

When everyone was seated, Mrs. Jordan asked, "Does anyone know something about our Student Council?"

Kevin raised his hand. "My brother was on it last year."

"What did he do?"

"I know he got out of class for meetings."

Alex laughed. "I'm for that!"

Mrs. Jordan smiled. "Kevin, do you know what happened at the meetings?"

"Once they planned a skating party for the whole school. My brother wanted to do a haunted house but he voted for what his class said they wanted."

"Did they just plan things for kids to have fun?" asked Mrs. Jordan.

"No, they collected toys and winter clothes for poor kids."

"I remember," said Kristen. "Mom took me to the store and let me pick out a toy and a book to give. It felt good knowing a girl who doesn't have very many things would have something really nice. We got some socks and underwear, too."

"Underwear!" Holly rolled her eyes. "Who'd want someone to give them underwear?"

"I thought that, too," said Kristen, "but it's important for a family who doesn't have much money."

The children talked until no one had any more questions. Then Mrs. Jordan asked who wanted to be on the Student Council. Lots of hands went up. Mrs. Jordan wrote names on the board.

"We'll vote by secret ballot. That's how your parents vote in an election." Mrs. Jordan passed paper. "Write the names of two class-mates. Your representatives will vote for what you tell them you

want. After each meeting they will tell us what they did."

"May we vote for ourselves?" asked Lexie.

"I bet the president voted for himself!" said Luke.

"I'm sure he did," said Mrs. Jordan. "Yes, Lexie, if you really want the job, you should vote for yourself."

"But if you want parties," said Holly, "vote for me!"

Katie, Bob, and Tyler counted the votes. "Holly and Kevin are our representatives," said Bob.

Everybody clapped, even the kids who hadn't won.

"Congratulations," said Mrs. Jordan. "Your first meeting is next Monday at two o'clock."

"Lucky!" Luke whispered to Kevin. "You get to skip math class."

Kevin grinned. "Yes, but I bet I'll have it for homework."

Jump Rope Games

Life, Liberty, and the Pursuit of Happiness
Everyone has the right to do things that make them happy, as long as they do not harm the rights of others.

"Let's ask Dori to jump rope with us," said Kristen.

"I won't be happy if she plays," said Holly.

"She has a right to be happy, too," said Zoe.

"She came from another school," Holly said. "She probably doesn't know our rhymes."

"We can teach her," said Zoe.

"Then she'll want to be in our club. I bet she doesn't even have yellow socks."

"So?" said Amanda.

"Let's vote," said Kristen.

"We don't have to vote!" Holly kicked some stones with the toe of her shoe. "You all want her to play, so OK."

She walked over to Dori. "Want to jump rope with us?" she asked.

Dori's face lit up. "Thanks," she said.

"You'll be all-time twirler." Holly handed one end of the rope to Dori and the other end to Kristen. "I'm first," she said and began to chant.

> *A my name is Alice.*
> *My husband's name is Arthur.*
> *We come from Alaska,*
> *and we have an alligator.*

Holly skipped out and Amanda jumped in. Dori and Kristen twirled.

B my name is Brandi... Amanda's foot tangled in the rope. She reached for Dori's end.

"Take Kristen's end, Holly said. "Dori is all-time twirler." When the bell rang Zoe looped the rope around her arm. "Thanks for twirling, Dori. I hope you liked it."

"It was fun to see how you play," said Dori. "At my old school we used two ropes. And we turned them in different directions."

"Cool!" said Amanda. "Could you show us?"

"I don't know," Dori said. "It's pretty hard to teach somebody when I'm all-time twirler."

"Oh," said Holly, "that was just for today!"

Jared Takes Cuts

Equality
All people should have equal rights and opportunities.

"Hey, go to the back," Luke said as Jared stepped into line in front of him.

"Alex will give me cuts. Won't you, Al?"

"I don't care," Alex answered, "as long as you're behind me."

"See," said Jared.

"No fair!" Luke pushed Jared.

Mrs. Jordan came up to them. "What's going on, boys?"

"Jared cut into the line!" said Luke.

Mrs. Jordan looked thoughtful. "I call you by groups so everyone can be first sometime. Is it your turn, Jared?"

Jared scuffed his toe on the floor. "No. But Alex let me take cuts."

"Jared always cuts to the front of the line!" said Luke.

Mrs. Jordan touched Jared's arm. "What do you think you should do?"

"OK, OK!" Jared got out of the line.

"Who cares about being first?" said Tyler. "Our gym class won't start until we're all there anyway. Those at the front of the line just wait longer."

Alex glared at Luke. "And now, since you made a fuss about it, we'll all be late and miss some of our gym time."

"It's the idea," said Luke. "Everyone is supposed to have equal rights! I don't want to give up some of mine so someone else can have more!"

The Student Council

Truth
Our government and citizens have a duty to be honest and trustworthy

On Monday, Kevin and Holly went to the library for the Student Council meeting.

Holly sat next to a girl who had been in her class the year before. "Hi, Brittany," she said.

Mr. Ward greeted the students. "Congratulations on being elected to the Student Council. It's an honor. But it also has responsibilities. Together we'll plan activities for our school and our community. You must think not just what you want, but also what other students in your class want."

Holly raised her hand. "I told my class I'd vote for parties."

Mr. Ward smiled. "Then since they elected you, they'll expect you to vote for parties."

A girl raised her hand. "Last year the Student Council had a harvest festival. Could we do that this year?"

"Or how about an all school sleepover?"

"And we could make holiday pies for the homeless shelter."

"Those are all good ideas," said Mr. Ward. "We can do whichever ones you want."

"Let's have the harvest festival first," suggested a boy. "We can ask everyone who comes to pay and use the money for our next project."

"That's a good idea," said Kevin.

Mr. Ward asked them to vote. Most children voted for the harvest festival. They picked a Friday night in October. They decided to have games, food, and a pumpkin contest.

"At our next meeting we'll work in groups called committees," said Mr. Ward. "Each committee will do one thing for the harvest festival. Tell me what you want to work on."

Brittany turned to Holly. "I like making posters. Let's sign up for that."

"OK," said Holly.

When they went back to class, Kevin and Holly told about the meeting. The class agreed the harvest festival would be fun.

The next day Brittany met Holly on the playground. "I told my teacher our committee would have extra meetings to make posters. Why don't you tell your teacher, too?"

"But Mr. Ward said we'd work at the next Student Council meeting," said Holly.

Brittany rolled her eyes. "Don't you get it? We can get out of more classes if we say we need more time."

"OK. Let's meet tomorrow after lunch." Holly giggled. "That's when my class has social studies."

"Ask your teacher for poster paper and markers," said Brittany. "I"ll get some stuff, too."

The next afternoon Brittany and Holly spread their papers on the hallway floor. Brittany drew a horse.

"What's that got to do with the harvest festival?" asked Holly.

"Nothing," said Brittany. "I like horses."

Holly drew a pumpkin. "I think we should stick to what we said we'd do."

"Go ahead," said Brittany. "I'll do a poster after this." She picked a glitter pen and drew stars on the horse's saddle.

The girls talked while they drew. Holly looked at the clock. "It"s almost time for my class to have music." She put the markers in their box.

Brittany put the glitter pens in her pocket.

"Are those yours?" asked Holly.

"They are now," said Brittany. "I don't have any like them at home."

"But they are school supplies," said Holly.

"I think we deserve something for our work on the harvest festival," said Brittany. "Besides, my teacher won't miss them. She has more."

Holly went back to her classroom. She put the markers on the supply shelf. She wondered if she should tell Mrs. Jordan about Brittany and the glitter pens. She didn't want to get her friend in trouble, and besides, it hadn't been a real committee meeting. Maybe she'd get in trouble, too.

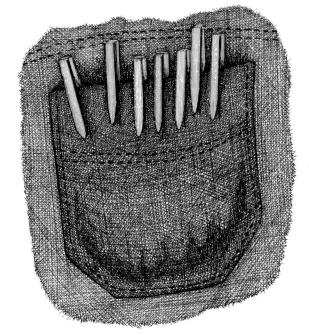

A Playground Problem

The Common Good
Each of us has a duty to work together to improve our communities and our country

"Wow! Our playground looks terrible!" Kevin said.

"Yeah," said Jared. "It's those big kids who come here after school to shoot hoops. They throw their candy wrappers and junk on the ground."

"Why?" asked Luke.

"They say it's the janitor's job to pick up stuff," said Jared.

"I bet they wouldn't like to clean up after other people," said Kevin.

"Someone should build a fence," Bob said, "with a gate that locks."

"And barbed wire on top so no one can climb over," said Jared.

"Who'd do it?" asked Kevin.

"How about the Student Council?" asked Luke. "You're our representative."

"The Student Council doesn't have any money yet. We need this done now."

"Maybe the Board of Education," said Bob. "They must have money."

"OK," said Kevin. "Let's write them a letter."

"They'll never go along with the barbed wire," said Luke.

"I was just kidding," said Jared.

"And if there's a locked gate, we won't be able to play after school either," said Bob.

Luke frowned. "The lady who has the day care down the street brings little kids here, too. They shouldn't play in this mess. They'll probably get germs or something."

"What about making it easy to throw away trash?" said Bob. "My mom carries a bag for my sister and me to use."

"Can we borrow your mom?" Jared joked.

Luke laughed. "Or at least her bag?"

"How about trash cans?" said Bob.

Jared's cap blew off. He stepped on it to catch it. "Trash cans are a good idea, but they'd have to be heavy enough not to blow over in the wind."

"Or be knocked over by a dog."

"They should be big, like the ones in the park!" said Bob.

"Let's ask Mrs. Chavez if we can tell our idea to the principal," said Luke.

The boys went to the playground aide. "We have an idea to clean up our playground," said Kevin. "May we go in and talk to Mr. Hamilton?"

"We sure need a good idea," said Mrs. Chavez. "Your ticket in from the playground is one piece of trash."

"That's another good idea!" said Kevin. Each boy grabbed some litter and took it inside.

Mr. Hamilton nodded as he listened. "Good thinking," he said. " Write your letter to the Board of Education I'll ask them to talk about it at their next meeting."

"Mrs. Jordan will let us write our letter in class," said Kevin.

"We'll get other kids to help clean up," said Bob.

"We'll have a litter patrol!" said Jared.

A few days later Mr. Hamilton called the boys to his office. " Well, guys, you did it! I told the Board how you used your recess time to clean up the playground. They liked your letter. They are proud of you for thinking about everyone who comes here to play. We can pick out trash cans, and they will pay for them."

"Hooray!"

The boys and Mr. Hamilton gave high-fives all around.

It's Not Fair

Justice
Everyone should be treated fairly by our rules. Sometimes what is fair is not equal.

Truth
We have a duty to be honest and trustworthy.

"Are you done with your math already?" Lexie whispered.

"Yes." Jessica answered.

"Your paper doesn't look done."

"I did four problems." Jessica shoved her book in her desk.

"Mrs. Jordan said. . ."

"Tyler's only doing four, so I did four."

"But Tyler has a broken arm!"

"We're all in the same class," Jessica said. "Remember? Mrs. Jordan talked about what's fair for one is fair for everybody."

"Yes, but I think she wants us to do the whole page."

"Do it then. I'm done." Jessica put her paper in the basket on Mrs. Jordan's desk. She went to the game corner.

Soon the whole class was whispering. Luke and Dori turned in their papers and went to play with Jessica. Some children went to the reading rug. Others got out markers and drawing paper.

After recess Mrs. Jordan said, "Boys and girls, many of you turned in math papers that weren't finished. Will someone tell me why?"

The children wiggled in their seats.

Alex raised his hand. "Jessica said we didn't have to."

"Really?" Mrs. Jordan seemed surprised.

Luke nodded. "She said Tyler was only doing four and what's fair for one is fair for everybody."

Mrs. Jordan's voice was soft. "Is that why some of you didn't do all the problems?"

"Yes," the children said.

"We did talk about fairness when we made class rules," said Mrs. Jordan. "I wonder if this is the same."

"I think it's different," said Holly. "I did the whole page."

"I know you did. How is it different?"

"Tyler has a broken arm," said Lexie.

"Does that matter?" asked Mrs. Jordan.

"Yes," said Bob. "If he did the whole page with his left hand, he'd be here till midnight."

"But he won't learn as much as we will if he doesn't do the same work," said Jessica.

"That's true," said Mrs. Jordan.

Tyler looked sad. "I'd do more if I could."

Mrs. Jordan nodded.

"I could write his paper for him when I'm done with mine," said Alex.

"Me, too," said some other children.

"That's very kind of you. But if no one helps him, is it fair for Tyler to have less work?" asked Mrs. Jordan.

"Yes!" The children agreed.

"OK" Mrs. Jordan smiled. "Now let's work on the papers

that need to be finished."

Holly walked up to Mrs. Jordan's desk. "Since I did the whole math page, may I work on my poster for the harvest festival?"

Mrs. Jordan nodded.

Holly bit her lip. "Brittany and I didn't really have a committee meeting the other day."

"Her teacher and I wondered about that."

"I'm sorry I lied."

"Thank you for telling me." Mrs. Jordan squeezed Holly's hand. " Help yourself to the supplies you need."

The Key Mystery

Patriotism
We all have a duty to serve each other and our country.

"Did you ever wonder why our school is called Key Elementary?" asked Mrs. Jordan.

"It's a mystery to me!" said Bob.

The class laughed.

"What do you think?" Mrs. Jordan asked.

"Maybe somebody found a key here, like to a pirate's treasure chest," said Bob.

Lexie giggled. "I don't think they'd name a school for that."

Kevin said, "If something like that had happened, we'd know about it."

"Yes," said Tyler. "The pirate's chest would be in the showcase by the front door!"

"Do you know?" asked Jessica.

Mrs. Jordan nodded.

"Then tell us!" said Tyler.

"It will be more fun if you find out for yourself."

"Like solving a mystery," said Luke. "Will you give us a clue?"

"Have you read what it says above the front door?" Mrs. Jordan asked.

Jared stood up. "I'll go look."

"Take a pencil and paper with you to copy what you find."

"Maybe the school is like a key in some way," said Holly.

"The key to learning!" said Katie.

The class groaned.

"My dad would say that," said Katie.

Mrs. Jordan smiled. "Very good. What other ideas do you have?"

The class kept on talking.

Jared burst through the door. "Francis Scott Key! That's what it says over the front door." He handed Mrs. Jordan his paper.

"Good, Jared." She wrote the name on the board.

"That must be someone's name," said Luke.

"Maybe a teacher, or the principal," said Dori.

Holly shook her head, "We know all of them."

"I mean a long time ago, when the school was built."

"Maybe it's someone famous," said Amanda.

Tyler got out of his seat. "I'll look in the encyclopedia."

He pulled a book from the shelf and turned pages. "Here it is! Francis Scott Key!"

Other kids crowded around. Tyler read out loud:

"He became famous for writing the words of *The Star - Spangled Banner* during the War of 1812. Key was on a boat in Baltimore harbor the night the British attacked Fort McHenry. In the morning he saw the flag was still flying. That meant the fort had not surrendered. Key wrote a poem to show his joy. In 1931 his poem became the national anthem of the United States."

"So that's who our school is named for!" Zoe said.

"The song is played whenever Americans want to show their love for our country," said Mrs. Jordan.

"Like at ball games!" said Bob.

Mrs. Jordan pushed a button on her CD player. The music started. The children sang:

> *O say, can you see, by the dawn's early light,*
> *What so proudly we hail'd at the twilight's last gleaming?*

Whose broad stripes and bright stars, thro' the perilous fight,
O'er the ramparts we watch'd were so gallantly streaming?
And the rockets' red glare, the bombs bursting in air,
Gave proof thro' the night that our flag was still there.
O say, does that star-spangled banner yet wave
O'er the land of the free and the home of the brave?

When the song ended Kevin said, "Freedom is important to Americans. Many people have fought and died for it."

Bob put three fingers to his forehead and saluted the flag. "I won't think of it as just the baseball song anymore!"

Adoption Day

Diversity
Our different backgrounds helped build this country and make it stronger.

Jared held the classroom door open for Katie. "Thanks, Jared." She slid the box she was carrying onto the table. "Mrs. Jordan, these are cookies for the class."

"How nice," said Mrs. Jordan. "We'll enjoy the treat."

"Is it your birthday?" asked Lexie.

"No, it's my Adoption Day."

"What's that?" asked Bob.

"It's the day my mom and dad brought me from China."

"Do you remember living in China?"

"No. I was just a baby."

"So, are you Chinese or American?" asked Jared.

"I'm both. I was born in China, but I'm a citizen of the United States."

"Was it hard to become a citizen?" asked Zoe.

"I became a citizen as soon as I was adopted, because my parents are citizens."

"I wonder," said Mrs. Jordan, "if any of you know what countries your ancestors came from."

"My grandfather told me his grandparents came from Germany," said Kevin. "They had to go through Ellis Island in New York."

"My family is part English and part Irish," said Jessica.

Bob said, "Mine is Polish, Russian, and Finnish."

"I know I'm part Ojibwa Indian and part French," said Luke.

"My mother made a family tree," said Dori. "She found out some of our relatives came over on the *Mayflower*!"

"All of you may have interesting stories about the history of your families," said Mrs. Jordan.

"Let's find out and tell the class," said Kevin.

"My grandma will let me bring in some of her pictures," said Kristen, "and she makes Swedish cookies."

"Yum!" Tyler patted his stomach. "Could we have a special day to bring in stuff and tell about it?"

"Good idea," Mrs. Jordan agreed.

"We could call it Adoption Day," said Kevin, "because someone in our family came from another country and adopted the United States as home."

"We could make a map—"

"And we can dress in costumes—"

"And bring special food—"

"Stop!" Mrs. Jordan laughed and held up her hand. "One at a time, please." She made a list on the board.

For two weeks the class worked on their projects at home and at school. They decorated the classroom with flags of other countries.

They filled tables and shelves with family keepsakes.

On Adoption Day Amanda wore a white cap, an apron, and wooden shoes. "My ancestors came from Holland. They were farmers. Wooden shoes kept their feet dry."

Tyler had on a black coat and a white shirt. He tucked his pant legs in his socks and put on a cap. "My great-great-grandfather was from Hungary." He held up a needle and thread. "He was a tailor. He sewed clothes."

"So you're Tyler the tailor!" said Alex.

Jared told the class, "I found out I have ancestors from seven countries. My dad said the United States is called a melting pot. That's because people from all over the world work and live together."

Zoe said, "My mother says our country is like a stew. People brought customs from where they lived before. Each one added something different that makes America what it is."

When it was Katie's turn she uncovered a plate of cooked rice wrapped in seaweed. She gave some to everyone.

"It's good!" said Jared.

"Even though I don't remember China," said Katie, "I'm proud to be a Chinese American."

"And," said Mrs. Jordan, "we're glad you shared your adoption story with us so we could learn about our heritage."